OCEAN
IT'S MY HOME!

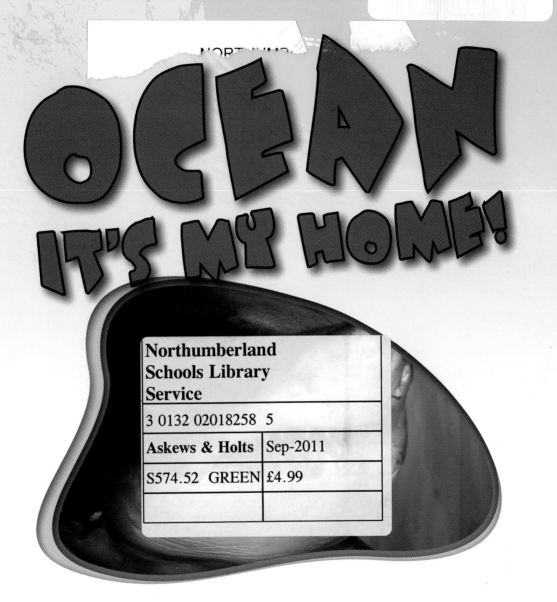

Angela Royston

Published 2011 by
A&C Black Publishers Ltd.
36 Soho Square, London, W1D 3QY

www.acblack.com

ISBN   HB 978-1-4081-3376-7
       PB 978-1-4081-3371-2

This book is produced using paper that is made from wood grown in managed, sustainable forests. It is natural, renewable and recyclable. The logging and manufacturing processes conform to the environmental regulations of the country of origin.

Produced for A&C Black by Calcium. www.calciumcreative.co.uk

Printed and bound in China by C&C Offset Printing Co.

All the internet addresses given in this book were correct at the time of going to press. The author and publishers regret any inconvenience caused if addresses have changed or sites have ceased to exist, but can accept no responsibility for any such changes.

Acknowledgements

The publishers would like to thank the following for their kind permission to reproduce their photographs:

Cover: Shutterstock
Pages: Dreamstime: Tom Dowd 8, Halbrindley 19, J. Henning Buchholz 15, Vladimir Seliverstov 18, Tyneimage 20, Vladvitek 1, 13, Willtu 12; National Geographic: Norbert Wu/Minden Pictures/N G Stock 11; Photolibrary: Franco Banfi 16, Corbis 21, Doug Perrine 9, Wolfgang Poelzer 3, 14, Tom Soucek 17; Rex: Nature Picture Library 10; Shutterstock: Rich Carey 6, Khoroshunova Olga 5, Specta 4, 7.

Contents

Water World

Lots of animals live in the **oceans**. Some are beautiful, others look very strange!

Swimming together

Lots of fish swim in the oceans. Some swim in huge groups, called **shoals**.

Keep together!

It is safer to swim as a group.

Crab home

Some sea creatures, such as crabs, hide under the sand.

Reef Home

Lots of animals live around **coral reefs**. A coral reef looks like a plant, but it is made up of lots of tiny animals.

Coral

Scary stinger

Sea anemones live on coral reefs. They have **tentacles** that sting.

This coral looks like a cauliflower!

Clownfish

An anemone's tentacles sting fish – except the clownfish.

Clownfish

Can't sting me!

Fantastic Fins

Fish use their **fins** to swim in their ocean home. Some fish have special fins.

Fish that fly

Flying fish use their fins to leap out of the sea and **glide** like a bird.

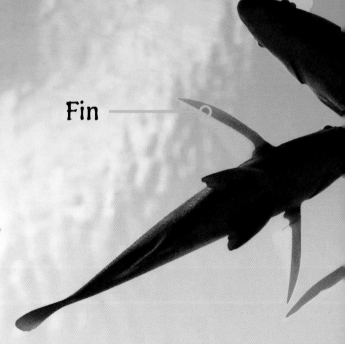

Fin

Flying fish can fly for 30 seconds.

We can fly!

Big fin

Fastest fish

A sailfish uses
its huge fin to
swim really fast.

In the Dark

Strange fish live at the bottom of the sea. It is always dark down here.

Look at my light!

An anglerfish uses its light to make fish swim close. Then it gobbles them up.

An anglerfish makes its own light.

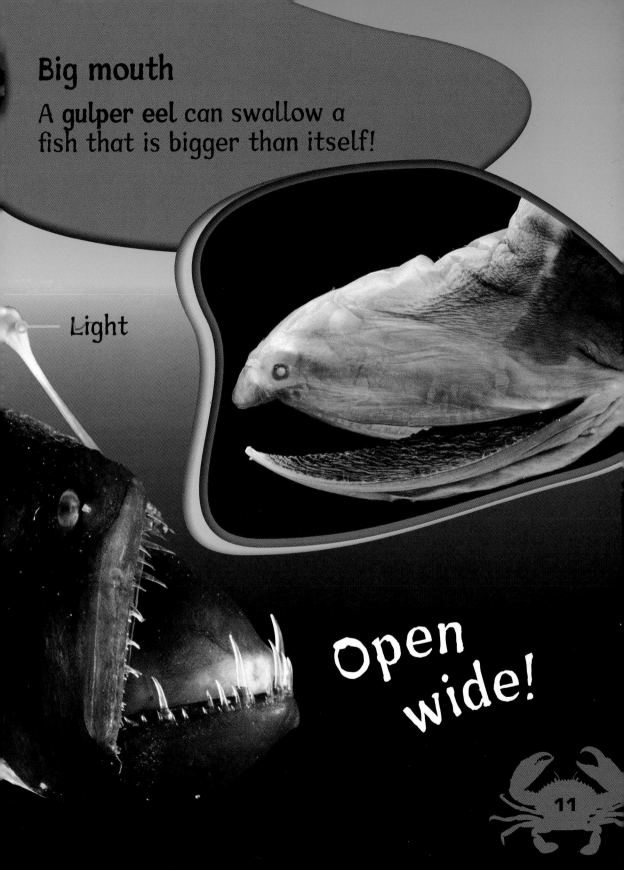

Big mouth

A gulper eel can swallow a
fish that is bigger than itself!

Light

Open
wide!

11

Shark!

Sharks are speedy swimmers. They hunt and eat fish and other sea animals.

Killer shark

The great white shark is one of the biggest and fastest sharks. It is also one of the scariest!

Fin

Great whites have a white belly.

White belly

Shiny new teeth

Every time a shark
loses a tooth, a new
one takes its place.

Scary shark

13

Water Wings

Rays are wide, flat fish.
They swim through water
by flapping their wings.

Giant ray

A ray has a long, thin tail. A giant
manta ray is the biggest ray of all.

We don't bite

Wing

Tail

No teeth

Manta rays have no
teeth. They swallow
tiny sea animals.

A manta
ray is big but
harmless.

Ocean Giants

Whales are huge. Blue whales are the largest animals on Earth.

Coming up for air

Whales swim underwater, but they come up to the surface to breathe in air.

Sing along!

Big breath

Whales blow out air and water, and then breathe in air.

Humpback whales sing as they swim.

Cold Home

Walruses live in cold and icy seas. They have lots of fat to keep them warm.

Long teeth

A walrus has two long teeth called **tusks.** It uses them to fight and to find food.

Walruses like to lie on ice.

Ice pick

A walrus uses its tusks to help it climb on to the ice.

Chill out!

Above the Sea

Some birds fly over huge oceans. If they get tired, they sleep as they fly!

Making a nest

Seabirds make nests on rocks and cliffs. They lay their eggs in them.

Puffins make nests on rocks.

Huge wings

Albatrosses glide for hours without moving their wings.

Rocky home

Glossary

albatrosses very large seabirds

coral reefs structures that feel like rock but are made of millions of tiny sea animals

fins parts of a sea animal that stick out from the animal's body. A sea animal moves its fins to help it to swim.

glide fly without moving the wings

gulper eel deep-sea fish with a very big mouth and a stretchy stomach

oceans huge areas of water

shoals large groups of fish

tentacles long feelers that a sea animal uses to move and to feel. Some tentacles contain stings.

tusks two long teeth, one on each side of the mouth

Further Reading

Websites

This website gives lots of facts about sharks. Find it at:
www.enchantedlearning.com/subjects/sharks

You can listen to the song of a humpback whale at:
www.youtube.com/watch?v=xo2bVbDtiX8

Books

Oceans and Seas by Nicola Davies,
Kingfisher (2004).

Pup to Shark by Camilla de la Bédoyère,
QED (2009).

Whales and Dolphins by Caroline Harris,
Kingfisher (2005).

Index